W9-ACH-931

FUGUE STATE

FUGUE STATE

Bill Berkson

Z

ZOLAND BOOKS

Cambridge, Massachusetts

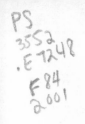

First edition published in 2001 by
Zoland Books, Inc.
384 Huron Avenue
Cambridge, Massachusetts   02138

FIRST EDITION

Cover painting: Yvonne Jacquette, *Mixed Heights and Harbor from World Trade
Center II*, 1998, oil on canvas, 79¼ X 58⅜ inches. Courtesy of the DC Moore
Gallery.

PRINTED IN THE UNITED STATES OF AMERICA

05 04 03 02 01   8 7 6 5 4 3 2 1

This book is printed on acid-free paper, and its binding materials have been
chosen for strength and durability.

Library of Congress Cataloging-in-Publication Data
Berkson, Bill.
Fugue state / Bill Berkson.
p. cm.
ISBN 1-58195-104-3 (pbk.)
I. Title

PS 3552.E7248 F84 2001
811'.54dc21   2001026136

Some of these poems and other pieces have appeared in the following chapbooks, magazines and anthologies: *A Copy of the Catalogue* (Labyrinth, Vienna, 1999), *New American Writing, Peninsula, o-blēk, The World, Café Review, Log, Angle, Up Late: American Poetry Since 1970, American Poets Say Goodbye to the 20th Century, Gate, B-City, Notus, Sugar Mule, The City Review, A Norton Anthology of Postmodern American Poetry, Out of This World, Broadway 2, Mudfish, Jacket, SFAI Eye, Mike & Dale's Younger Poets, Skanky Possum, Deadsnake Apotheosis, Arshile, Combo, Penumbra, Zyzzyva, Intent, Jejune, Milk, Subdream, Big Bridge, Lungfull!, Shiny, Euro-San Francisco Poetry Festival, [Melancholy Breakfast], Gare du Nord, Chicago Review, Cybercorpse, Grinning Corpse* and *Reading Jazz.*

"Purgatory" appeared as red lettering on a glass door in the exhibition *Otherworldly,* curated by Connie Wolf at the San Francisco Art Institute, 1999. "The Recital," "Graphics" and "By Halves" were published as broadsides by Pressed Wafer, the New College of California Book Arts Program, and by Steve Woodall for the San Francisco Center for the Book, respectively. "Stains of Stalin" was included in *The Blind See Only This World,* an anthology and set of broadsides honoring John Wieners from Pressed Wafer and Granary Books.

Thanks to the editors and designers of those publications.

Special thanks to Yvonne Jacquette, Adam DeGraff, Larry Thomas, Anne Waldman, the American Academy in Rome, Artspace, and the Fund for Poetry.

CONTENTS

On the Waldo Grade

Clerical Workers

A Copy of the Catalogue

Notes to the Poems

To Connie

On the Waldo Grade

A HEAD AT THE COVERS

I removed the rains and motored
and flipped through the covers of a board
a card with shavings labeled to a lace cross
in the mirror-narrow confines of an
eyesore fog you can fly
over still and put
your finger on a dune

as if pins were
to be pushed dimly
inches downward from
a manila star

What if the panic is on
and this parrot weather
has crow's-feet
which aren't a regular part of the job
but the deep end of a lot of things
that leak their loads like twigs to the vortex
an uphill travail

Unlivable sounds stem from the woodworks
traipse on the back of an igneous broom
that busses bees to certain rarity

but I'm with
the sun bolting
all the ledges
my odd blue dots anchored
I barely think to what
since what has gone and merged

The whole inch piles on gathered corks
the strips in place are a snore of blue
a while so lifted you watch it shatter care,
lacking evidence, with personnel to spare
I left a face spinning on the stair

SHELTER

to Jim Brodey

Do you recall the words to fog
or flotsam slipping legs into the laundry bag?

So many have left the human party
'twixt meats and jellies
that now seem pitched from chill couch ease.

Their message units stroll anelastic yet duly personable.

A jocular finality holds sway
at face value, like a multinational police force

sounding the twisty miles in tow,
some original mass remanded.

IN A HAND NOT MY OWN

A blank wall is singing
to be separate from the rest.
It is too mild for the casually attired
to be living among their glittery glassine poses.
Or else my superstitions are wrong,
built sideways from a limb, or anyhow panting.

But why fuss? If personality were legal tender,
ours would pass for coin of the realm. As
it is, not one will stir for
the detached, the slow dickering of affect
and demise leading to the dustbin at heart.

I speak volumes across the rim of a quail.
I glisten in footage to smother all currency
and as I crumble I succeed,
empire-elect of a most honorable science,
knowing the babble that toil concludes, condones.

MANDATE: ARCHIE TO JUGHEAD

I won't make another empty inventory
copied a hundred times across the board,
arsenal of declensions that never break the mold
with good reason inveigling
impulse to poem with no sad words.

A sonnet's about the size of human talk
slyly founded, with mirrored character in mind,
crotchety, melancholy, blue —
the landscape taken from a landscape we knew
taken for words, bearing their own stamped trees.

Then if I steer clear, combinations of earth
must bubble away, and in the death of the bandstand
you are bequeathed, catering a taste test
with white gloves in the sempiternal field house
gathered like hair down the back of a shirt.

Let them stick or be flushed.
Although the weather suffers generally without people,
the pale loiterer can still be found
in thinly managed time
plotted by the transverse —

a successful inoculation
at the gnome's wrought door,
having bypassed absorption and succinct betrayal,
that possessive rule we keep to a brain
as in: I stole your letter sweater.

THE OBVIOUS TRADITION

I haven't remembered anything, only the names
and that their dates have been replaced by fees
toted up out of mischief:
a whopping yellow sun, finesse swallowed hard,
a scrapbook in pantyhose dawdling beside some Shreveport-
      like expanse.

But now you see it, she's supposed to call.
Surely neither will converse, they merely tell,
succumbing to a disorderly shelf life like Tampax in June.
Salute the budding terminus where the East Side was.
Can there be a way to redefine the tense behind its jaunts,
the pubescent imagery a hand calls forth
as, rippling, it is thrust into the brine?

                    The phantom tugboat slips along
in depths past Garbo's awnings and the united glaze
which wilts, harnessing dim signatories in the windows' sarong.
Do things go further in need as I could? Or are they immune?
How else have I been taught to guess
and then been told to know, because matter equals good?
A silken light masks the entrance to the market proofs of time.

WAY HOW

Markets hit return
the egregious debauch
and in the garden

ever remotely broken car:
Contempt City at the bypass,
creasing good-natured binges.

The layouts of minus
squat on the rooftops
of princely Eden.

Wet jewels waxing into struts,
waltzes, thankful factory scraps,
hot potions brought in on trays —

the way it sounds at this end.

MELTING MILK

Do things then happen
despite our knowing
and is each misnomer

but a dream? Natural hiked-up
detail consciously
during years of anxious

foreshortening, now distanced
by tinsel, cup, ring, ball,
heart, horseshoe, snail,

acts like visibility
of tempos irreducible
to a fractious stance.

So find any plausible footing
and grab: Do we get to stay over?
"Sorry," says Recorded Time,

"didn't get it, lost
my concentration." First error:
the profile seen double

smoothes it out
and forklifts ballast. Verso,
enter nameless emptiness,

heavy on comparison, contingency,
conceit. How's it getting dark
because things line up in a

massive buddy system, a grab
bag of rimless data,
milking lights, red ball to green spool,

as we think.
Ash is crystal.
Ecstasy is near.

GRAPHICS

Epodes of bat in city streets
Sucrose end-alls spraying rural yards
Oil poured on the curious ear
Pressed against antibiotic, zero breast

Green gum and a dribble
Occlude in revision of clean pines
Overdone as expensive
Modulation and nubile fender drifts

Little light skims from the top
But there lies the clever ground
Usurped by the rightful observer
Restoring to us our vanity, his carte blanche.

ROY ELDRIDGE, LITTLE JAZZ

A hard look and a fake I.D. won't get you
into the Metropole, but at 15 you can stand under
the marquee's heat lamps outside to listen.

That epithetical "little" must've
implied something synedochial
together with a downright

brevity. Eldridge was his own quintessence:
as Billy Tenant expressed it, "the guy who
could squeeze anything out of a trumpet."

His playing contains no stunts or slurs.
Each bitten phrase meted out with compact dignity.
Where the trumpet blares, its pointed elevation —

 zigguratic high notes, chomps
goading (in Kenny Clarke, for one) a concomitant
reach in rhythm (the ride cymbal rose

in prominence) —
with an aspiration like the Chrysler Building
clinches the night air.

FUGUE STATE

Worth mentioning?
The horizon, such as is, splits mind across the middle.
To turn in this world first: mirage
of motel swale, votary albumens checked in coils, an ionosphere
    of certain age.
The check is in the mail. When this arrives, millions cash in.
Gone with its physics, the downy mist from motor inn planks.
("Once I chased that same white vapor down a soft shoulder near
    the Music Tent.
It must have been a singular joy to spy at dawn beyond to stand
    deep still and feed the stains. Signed, Do Tell.")
It so happens, what chemically will invoice time to a rug shack.
Gone tree, the alder now a gilded stump. The gridlock rose has
    mattered more to some
with less and less to tune, please notice the smallness pending there.
That species worth mentioning?
It will all return to fugue.

Say to yourself I used to.
Let me count the ways to say I don't.
Sexual union once was a paradigm.
The '80s, though, afforded little random socializing.
To operate both as a family and work at home, how many phones
    do you require?
As in a fatalistic French movie circa 1957-1962, the plot element
    creasing a white linen suit,
who taught you to smoke and drink and carry on like that?

Amateur self always swapping cartoon bodies —
not to mention the abstract wisps spilt in recollection's meadows,
house guesses plaited with resumable, squat truths —

14

haven't you felt Mighty Mouse's female counterpart (can't think
of her name) lean on you
with lips of high-gloss ginkgo dew?
A seed bag of gravels for her furs!
You take up a quill and inscribe the day's prophecies in nomen-
clature without apex.
Beneath fumes, the project turns to swatting the states upon
the hump.
This visibility is notably perfect.
I apportion whomever crosses under the lintel, but ever it falls
to me.
Gone are the states.

"Arise, Sir Knight."

Whom do you most admire?
What is your least favorite egg concoction?
Which preposition best exemplifies a grassy ridge the likes of
which you see
tantamount to yellow, desirous, resinous, albeit past all mention?
Can you actually write in the dark by hand?
Commit each folly? Tear down advance notice?
The plums fall, nicked by stingers.
A feather squeaks in the leaves.
Tuna leap from the ocean at 360 degrees.
The more alert among us sit up and take notice.
Echoes in the machine part company.
One by one, the prawns mounted the barfly's plate.

The past is a blur.
Perhaps its task requires some special knowledge, feeding afresh
on what is
already given, a history of unintentional deletion embedded in its
own epoch-making pause.

Oh yeah? But, hush:
the letters wait on each vocable in the halls of permanent digress.
They jangle, frowsed in mint, whole mounds of ends.
Letter of detriment the silhouette won't resist.
Stupid language.
The car is ready, I rise, scaling Everest.

A stone leaf.
As monetary as teeth.
The box pictures the box.

There is just the mold (or mould?) of appearance proffered by a
    jelly jar.
There are administrations more average in a cup.
Bring on the menace, lest we euphemize the while . . .
The air smacks, understanding little and bilious.
It should learn to read.
But there is too much meaning to leave us from meaning more.
(I finally heard and closed the book for fear.)
Something characteristically physical lifts its hind foot.
How many deletions are still to be made?
All that seems is substituted for on the inside out.
And how will I know such shifted givens, O custodians far
    from home?
When you leave the building, things suspend from here.

AN EXAMPLE, WORTHWHILE

Single-point perspective got fudged.

The bird in the house flies in the eye of the god

Lounging at length across the field, a simple song.

One has to envision language or it's no help.

Know history backwards.

Lay into life.

A FINIAL

I can see where the sky takes a bend that the fogbank
hasn't blunted. I see the drawers pulled out
for access to same. If you are so inclined, matter can
be sensitive to the need for a shove.
I feel the finesse of particles at hand.
The origins of shape stare out from indelicate depths
where subjectivity can't follow, spilling itself.
Evidently, perhaps.

Clerical Workers

DEAR CONSUMER, THE ESTIMATE IS HIGH

The accountable imprints of the Grim Reaper
will have to be sponged off as click-click
the color wheel spins, scratching an itch to
the left of my shoe and staying an instant the
untoward of loss. An importunate diary
has had it thus, whose neighbors
imbibe the shanks of emotional tact
in which conviviality is depicted in ten
directions at once, and it just goes to show

the itch disappears with a toothpaste grin
that just goes to show you expressed some
consternation as to its ancient character's
surface tension in a cup rattled by traffic as you
write the check in folly at the perimeter
of this needless star

ENOUGH ALREADY

Time I do and if I don't
That particular wall seems tireless
Start a verb through the motions
The motions all ring true

What I didn't see or do it says double
In the proffered ranks of brim and arc
Ever verging on a world at bay
Tended-to as take-home pay

CLERICAL WORKERS

We have costs below our limitations
and worries meted out for those who demur
to pull their weight. The market is fixed.
And hell is versed in stains
and bifurcation spells an edge
flat-footed in the afternoon movie.
In this case, the lady's dress
feels serviceable and sticky as a Peter Paul's Mounds.

Another pretty face fakes out the scenery,
candlelit:
Mother knows you're nice but not how much you lie.

There is no percentage that comes from being set in Utopian ways.
All our assistants have passed through accredited points
where the assailants yearn,
gone slack.

Please, we will bring command to your private rooms.
Candies by the switchboard tell of management misfires
communicable by union, cubicle, slap, or chill.

AN EXAMPLE, VOLUNTEER BASIS

From dull beginnings
as when a thunderclap comes frowning
slop air wedged a light hail

to resistance and scandal
ditto the caveat
1 to 15 years at K-through-12 promises a monograph
          or has the blind door been jimmied?

Here in the city, pregnant, realistic,
clangorous empowerments of next move
(a dribble gloss at best) apropos alternate paths

Reevaluate thrush concept:
If only we knew, chaos dynamics would show
the Garden of Delights to be pulsing under a stoop at risk

but when drool impends
individual compliance goes home
to the flashy new inference paints.

EXPANDED X

The modus operandi of
an in-house relativist is
first to flirt with
his thought.

Ergo *Magnificat*:
enter spears in
gross abundance.

Whilst government threatens
try to make presence severe or
else wag
features accordingly.

MERZBAU

for Trevor Winkfield

The pieces had been milled, stacked, stitched, taken from various piles and then assembled at some distance in a perpendicular fashion, mostly. Before he got there, they were pulled apart. Did he color them before reassembling? Atilt, they "room" the viewer. The new construction feels endlessly banged together. The colors might keep you from hitting your head.

BRUNCH

All eyes were set upon
the suspected lady-killer
Claus Von Bulow and his tall
companion, the woman in
immense fur hat
across the table, until
late for her brunch date,
into Mortimer's strode
young, blond, tan Mrs. Pulitzer —
and smitten, Von Bulow to
the room at large declared:
"My God, I've been upstaged!"

TARPS

Modern sculpture, the wreck, embraces
inebriations of Khan.

Gosh, look, Walt, they are laying
track on Market for the Muni

in this town of white and pastel girls.

Sandwich yourselves, for appointments suck. My clothes
un- or overencumbered in drawers must strike the set.

Surreptitious self is it.
We don't want "It."

Between door and post obtains
an arithmetic.

SAINT SIR FRANCIS DARK

Words exchange places with the names for trees.

In the novelty of these moons,
A fair hair is worth its weight.

THE READER'S LOVER

Cannibals
A Marxist is cannibals.

The Former Ambassador
If we could talk on the 'phone one day, all of this could be unraveled.

Ten-Dollar Words
I am a product of my time.
Sociopolitical grief is the name
in anybody's book.

The Forest Folk
Patrimony sings!
Opera! Infinitude!

Half Man, Half Beast
One man, one beast.

LATE CAPITAL

Instruction blocks the curve
on the paper mountain, beside the mojo bus
of a chartreuse tint that neither art nor nature
can ever pretend to know,

                        exponentially.
A needle passes down material slopes
conceived of in
the crucible of a side path,
the bank of a weed, last capital
indicator —
and which little raccoon is yours?

ALL MY SONGS COME UNANNOUNCED

Holidays, you get your car washed.

The hockey games, the dickering puck.

Crazy lady scuffs cement at the base of a former hill.

Prices slashed: "We wuz rooked but good!"

And the gone frog hollers "Limits!"

What didn't happen once?

IN GRAY SWEATS

1.
A hidden logic exemplifies
stasis turnabout approximate to mildewed VCR
concentrated scenery pours
(Samson in the guise of Joe Camel grasps the lion on Trump's
     pediment)
where equity recedes
and her mandorla deepens
taking directions in terms of efficient daylight
vacuum motor fulminating
hair caught on a bus thrown back
theory each millennium propounds
in loops that recur
that an O-ring may need inserting at the Fed

2.
Artemisia Gentileschi supersedes Joe Blow
painters are the first to go
they put up the details roadside,
the likes of which a squashed pink balloon with a bright girl
     inside it, a whiffle
ball, rarified vehicles and gates, yellow hydrant, my camp
     moccasins fouled
all things pigmented, bookish and nerdy
practicalities under flannel skies
sensation argues a metalanguage
predictable glass charge, serve with sediment, mentia
in whose poems we carouse, por favor, swimmingly

3.
Facets of rank, appetition, attitude
dreams of status spearhead ebullience loss

our communal check deposited in advance of payment
the plans arisen like nothing we've ever seen, dark star
and I am glad to know of them
thriving in this sizzled atmosphere
where thought exchanged persons
for the long haul

Cover me

a rouged-over tetrahedron bestride the poop deck
ten little *indios*, whomp! a dark picture of a waterfall
enquiry into the origins of our ideas concerning the sublime,
        the beautiful, the mind/body split
a nonsense split
since this is the sum, the share-the-never ennui lapse.

BINDING GRIEVANCE

Relief filled with donors
appetition skips a day, an hour.
Impressive muscles grow among
the hilly routes between.

This is your interim contract.

In the undertow, as Winslow
Homer saw it, Miss
Liberty negotiates her wits,
a core problem that functions
primly. The diverse throng suited up.

Everyone is a kind of Miss Liberty as far as
the powers that can be seen.

Line at denuded salad bar
slows: key under mat;
oxygen beds; summer,
pianissimo woman.

After the dust had settled
between speeches,
classes will resume.

Call us back with your name,
or could you do without?

A Copy of the Catalogue

FOR JIM GUSTAFSON

Last Words

"That's the way it goes."

"More light, please."

"Whose side are you on anyway?"

"Goodnight, sweet Prince."

"Shut the door on your way out."

"You want I should call you a cab?"

Gimme A Swig

There must have been a saturation of enchantment
at some point before the crafty badgers
dismantled their catch, the Actual, for
meathead determinism, pestilence futures, sub-
dular glitches, *et alia*. You had plenty to read,
a river slipping, sliding gently through it
every day, the first pineapple.

Vibrato came from Lee Wiley, Judy Garland told your correspondent in 1960, while listening to an old 78 rpm pressing of Lee's "Give It Back to the Indians."

SIGNATURE SONG

Bunny Berigan first recorded "I Can't Get Started"
with a small group that included Joe Bushkin, Cozy Cole
and Artie Shaw in 1936.
Earlier that same year, the song,
written by George Gershwin and Vernon Duke,
and rendered as a duet patter number by Bob Hope and Eve
Arden, made its debut on Broadway in *The Ziegfield Follies*.
By 1937, when Berigan re-recorded it in a big-band setting,
"I Can't" had become his signature song,
even though, within a few months, Billie Holiday would record
her astonishing version backed
by Lester Young and the rest of the Basie Orchestra.

Lovers for a time, Wiley and Berigan began appearing
together on Wiley's fifteen-minute CBS radio spot,
Saturday Night Swing Club, in 1936.
But in 1939, when Wiley recorded her album of Gershwin songs,
both Berigan and "I Can't Get Started" were absent from the set.
Berigan died from alcoholism-related causes on June 2, 1942.
Although "I Can't Get Started" is perfectly suited to Wiley's
deep phrasing and succinct vibrato, she recorded the ballad only
once, informally, in 1944, during a Los Angeles club date.
The Spanish Civil War started in 1936 and ended in 1939
with Generalissimo Francisco Franco's forces entering Madrid.
"I've settled revolutions in Spain" goes the line of Duke's
    lyric, just as odd.

A COPY OF THE CATALOGUE

★★★★★

Red Harvest: a property filmed by RKO circa 1933 as a musical comedy with a gangster subplot.

Red Harvest, starring Marlon Brando as the Continental Op, directed by Bernardo Bertolucci, shelved.

Red Harvest: Marlon Brando *is* the Continental Op in this film version of Dashiell Hammett's novel, directed by James Bridges, who died before filming could begin.

Dashiell Hammett's *Red Harvest*, most excellent film-to-be.

I will end with a lapse.

For an untitled chair, culture, culottes, Charlotte Corday, Robert Cordier & Eileen Corder, rec' room, Charlotte Rampling, Sock & Buskin, "Buckle down, Winsocki!" — "Plato or comic books, I'm versatile," brewing coffee through a windsock, Paris-Orly, 1964

Paint settles on the support
arguing the art of *pittura*
into the ground, where it surfaces —
part color, all manner of light — along the edge
                given a proper viewing distance

— to converse in color: "the perfect figure of measurement in space and of restarting in time." Now there's a thought. The periwinkle garnished, the sperm bank. One befouled character recites imperialist atrocities while another regrets the impeccably tailored English suits his mater gave away to do-gooders during his stoned-out, hippy-dippy, bell-bottoms phase. Who didn't do what to whom? "I spit on you, Yankee dork!" Yet doubleness dogs our days only once the admissions committee attends the proconsul's clip under the clock at the Biltmore — oh, please. Protracted swoons. One of me's head decorates an insurgent's dull green pike, or its twin, as the young and restless storm the comfort zone, valiantly punching holes in my alpaca-lined, red velvet pup tent.

VOLITION

He follows words and puts his thing to them.
He chews the landscape to process.
He is strict and bound to stand.
He smacks of fill and compelling evidence.

The field guide says there's
        a pond up
                the fire road in
                        the birches.

He is known for judging the lights before they are put out.
On the ulterior of a live tree, a double door to you.
He wants to know what still hasn't happened.

SO I FLED

but he who's that's
the deposition
comes unglued
comradery
apportioned
versus "skills"
labors on

he orders a
talking teapot
grosses
the disunity
of tombs
facing
the glossies'
sole accompaniment

no whirl
so sampled
as leaks back
to him
who hears her
carved bone sleekness
only begin to tell
her chatter blue blame

after David Shapiro

787B Castro Street
San Francisco CA 94114

March 3, 1997

Dear James Elkins,

This is in response to your notice in "studio-notes" about people who have cried in front of paintings.

In 1978, given the pretext of appearing in a poetry festival, I visited Amsterdam for the first time. My main objective as a tourist was to see the Vermeers in the Rijksmuseum and the others at the Mauritshuis a short train trip away in the Hague. Among the works in Amsterdam I was especially looking forward to seeing the *Woman in Blue Reading a Letter* — to see that blue "in the flesh," as it were, in its bell-like configuration. There it was, and wonderful, in the tidy run of pictures along one wall that included also *The Little Street* and *The Love Letter.*

Although most of my sightseeing during that Dutch trip was done in the company of poet friends who were likewise appearing at the festival, I made a point of reserving the Rijksmuseum for time alone. A half hour or more passed among Vermeer's exactitudes and dreamy light. I worked my way from left to right, interrogating each of the three paintings until I felt I had found out everything that could be revealed on first encounter. With a sigh I turned to leave the gallery and was immediately confronted by a fourth picture by Vermeer I hadn't noticed or even suspected was in the room, the so-called *Milkmaid,* on a short wall next to the door. What caught my eye, straight on, was just a detail — the dark mouth of the pitcher and the skein of white extending downward from its lip. Widening, my glance took in the astonishing barrel of the woman projected against the splendid white wall. In the instant, I gasped, and my heart thus jolted produced a rush of tears. Nearly twenty years later, I recall the experience with wonder. *The Milkmaid* was absent from the group of Vermeers that came to Washington last winter. What would happen if I saw it again?

Perhaps this will prove helpful in your research. Speaking of which, I was able to catch only the last few minutes of your talk on Chinese and Western painting at the CAA, and I wonder if there is a text of that talk which you could send me, or, if published, direct me to. And if there's any more I can tell you about my Vermeer crying jag, please don't hesitate to ask.

Best, sincerely,

PURGATORY

You know how
when two red lights

flash in the rearview mirror
and it could be a cop or only another

motorist braking
in the opposite lane?

That's just the way it's been
with me, somewhat.

LOUNGE MUSIC
(air: "Timor Mortis Conturbat Me")

for Bernadette Mayer

What's it going to be?

What're you gonna do about it?

Roundly deluded.

What'll it be?

A HYRAX ON HER SHOULDER

Degustibus does as Porky knows
Blue Terpsichore, a laugh riot:
Fated radiance, a soundtrack pending, holds
What takes one away to logic from your arms
In foregonest night
Neither thimble of death nor congealing old-age creeps.

HISTORY AT NIGHT

for Kevin Killian

It happened in Roddy McDowall's New York apartment, the night
he gave a party for Judy Garland and a few good friends. It was also
the night of the Democratic Convention in Los Angeles. Central
Park West, July 11, 1960, respectively. Myrna Loy fresh from her
return to movie stardom in *From the Terrace*. Montgomery Clift
recuperating apace. Adlai Stevenson was supposed to be a shoe-in
as the Democrats' nominee for President of the United States.
Lauren "Betty" Bacall, an avid Adlai fan, had gone off alone to
Roddy's bedroom to watch the proceedings on TV. "Those sons of
bitches," growled Betty, appearing nonplussed in the doorway to
the living room. Judy was laughing and confiding, patting Monty's
knees. Stephen Sondheim listened and lifted and lowered his chin.
Carol Lawrence watched, starry-eyed, somewhat awestruck, and
Larry Kert wondered. No one knew much about John F. Kennedy
yet. All they could think was "Harvard" and "Boston Irish
Catholic." Judy drank Blue Nun liebfraumilch poured from the
tall, thin bottle she had brought in a black tote bag.

ANOTHER COFFEE, AFTER SAINT AUGUSTINE

Missouri Compromise, empty adit,
some drifter's peony shirt caught on a nail.

The crude pocket stalled on purpose,
upholding its endless, universal squawk.

We hear of natural gasses, referrals bland —
all elaborate pellets and vials of ourselves,

contents unknown, ineffable, speaking grittily
out of the corner of one mouth:

I've come off it, why don't you?

AFTER HEINRICH HEINE

The rose, the lily, the dove, the sun,
I loved each one in love's mad swoon.
I love them no more, I live alone.
The little one, fine one, pure and true —
Selfsame source of all love's flows —
Lily, dove, sun and rose.

STAINS OF STALIN

She knew him somewhere between five p.m. and the next day.
His gaucheries were dire and nimble as iron socks.
And they rang, likewise, suppurating as
A glow along the Silk Road, as she
Healed her brow in the hospitals of a book. A stiff life
Intervening in the parlors. And then the crunch. Luncheon is
    served
On the patio, I kiss your hand, Madame — the era echoed
Such aggravation! — inside the thatch, the tablecloth,
Implying steely-eyed ambiguities never completely foolish
    enough but
Subject to derisory forced laughter brought harshly to bear
On every mother's child, as well you and I both know,
As well as the heartless, neutral, vine-colored
Slabs we put them under —
Only, angry birds that we are, I forget just which.

CAMERA OBSCURA

Ditsy love or
flagrant disturbation,
our happy murk
abreast
in a paper room —

what approval rating
did these persons,
not to be dissuaded,
fidgetingly,
seek?

The slogan
in signature attire,
ameliorative, yet with no especial
absence to speak of, steps up to purchase
one packet steel wool.

THE RECITAL

for Eric Fonteneau

It is said that, late in life, Denis Diderot force-fed his wife Nanette a diet of R-rated poetry and fiction, including his own *Jacques the Fatalist,* as a cure for her feelings of moral superiority. Diderot read to Nanette morning, noon and night, and whenever the Diderots had company, Mrs. D. would recite to her visitors whatever she had just absorbed. Slowly but surely, the cure took. "Conversation doubles the effect of the dosage," in a letter to their daughter wrote Diderot.

LA POÉSIE BLANCHE

I'd been over this once before.
I came out here
and went again
later, to see what if
anything that had been was left.

Yes, it was, and all of a piece,
yet not much else, or less in point of fact
than then.
         I wouldn't want to have to
turn around and find myself passing what
might have remained there fully, no matter why, in the bargain.

MEMOIR BAY

Succumbed to the art houses' clunk, my Mae, my Max?
Pry open now the lowly owl pellet so as to peruse

Lap, the car talk, the Boston rat catcher, vigilance
Bones eclectic in the manor, blinkered in some slipper's cap,

A mole slide's third's tainted fab blue hoot avail,
Taint, tawny micros stippling about a ditch,

On the brain gold feed plaques
Blend, the unissued stamp.

Great British tendencies parade to scumble
For their prehensile bearing inside Arcady body's blowfish

Disallowed toe quirk inclusiveness to Vendôme sashay
Brag an indifference at heat junction attaché, "no dice."

Plug archaic sense as surefire grid or folkway guide?
Film flak for comportment over desuetude event flop?

Like Benito Mussolini astride his trike,
Cupid and Psyche like each other.

Here where longueurs make or break the rules,
Losing is precious, heartbreak cool.

Maybe what you had all along was a cold.
(Search this site for lip.)

The thing you are swallows greater the stirred-up vendor base.
The jungle wet with index flings back an outer-limit margin
    deal that stews process through its sieve.

The mar is hardly fatal so lets us sniff it at about street
Level. Blithely pressured, the stupendously straight barebacked
    waitress at the Right Bank Cafe, Elizabeth Ashley, said okay,
    you got it, seated.

BY HALVES

do limits build
both sweet and cruel
or over to you off at
your compass studies,
visor to odd angles perforated,
plumb to sky
to service mouthful signage in pearly
cantina load where squawks from a ceiling,
headed down the demon slopes
for work place, total their sheer
carbon feed on an average night
that at any guardrail slick nails the morphological in bins?
Thus backup wealth lifts an ancient spume, glowering with grammar
whose joined bronze gives pause,
erect lapse paging glory, when wing is rag.

NOTES TO THE POEMS

On the Waldo Grade

The Waldo Grade is a roughly mile-long incline of California Highway 101 on the Marin County side of the Golden Gate Bridge. In the opening sequence of Delmer Daves's film *Dark Passage*, Lauren Bacall drives down this grade, headed for San Francisco, with Humphrey Bogart, an escapee from San Quentin, hiding in her back seat.

Shelter
Jim Brodey, 1942–1993.

Anelastic, "relating to the property of a substance in which there is no definite relation between stress and strain." (*Webster's Collegiate Dictionary*, Tenth Edition, 1996)

The Obvious Tradition
"Garbo's awnings": Greta Garbo lived in a building on Fifty-Second Street, one side of which faced the East River; many of the windows on that side had long green awnings.

Melting Milk
"Didn't get it . . .": Recorded Time here is Edwin Denby in an aside during a tape recording of his poetry at Giorno Poetry Systems, December 11, 1974.

Roy Eldridge, Little Jazz
When Roy Eldridge died in 1989, Jack Clarke asked me to write something about him for Jack's magazine *Intent*. The Metropole was a large walk-in jazz club on Broadway during the 1950s, with a marquee out front and a long bar, on a stage behind which played various "all-star" groups, including musicians as diverse as Eldridge himself, Henry "Red" Allen, Cozy Cole and the Pima trombonist Russell "Big Chief" Moore.

Fugue State
"A disturbed state of consciousness in which the one affected seems to perform acts in full awareness but upon recovery cannot recollect the deeds." (*Webster's Collegiate Dictionary,* Tenth Edition)

Mighty Mouse was a superhero of 1940s animated cartoons.

Clerical Workers

Most of the poems in this set take as sources the ambient languages of various work places — light industry, the administrative offices of primary and secondary schools, a fine arts college and other institutions and/or conglomerates.

Brunch
Mortimer's, a popular, uptown Manhattan restaurant during the 1980s, drew an especially glittery crowd for Sunday brunch. The "Mrs. Pulitzer" in question was then involved in scandalous divorce proceedings in Palm Beach, Florida.

Binding Grievance
Winslow Homer's painting *The Undertow* can be seen in the Sterling and Francine Clark Institute, Williamstown, Massachusetts.

A Copy of the Catalogue

For Jim Gustafson
Jim Gustafson, 1949-1996, dear Detroit-Bolinas poet friend.

A Copy of the Catalogue
Much of the information regarding the vicissitudes of *Red Harvest* as a prospective film property came from James Bridges and Jack Larson during their visit to San Francisco in the early 1970s.

The lines on *pittura* refer to writings on that topic by Leon Battista Alberti, Samuel Y. Edgerton, Jr., and Erwin Panofsky's *Perspective as Symbolic Form.*

"787B Castro Street . . ."
At the 1997 annual meeting of the College Art Association in New York, the art historian James Elkins circulated a request for accounts by people who had cried in front of paintings. This response was sent but never acknowledged.

Lounge Music
The "air" accompanying this poem is the refrain from Walter Savage Landor's "Lament for the Makers."

A Hyrax on Her Shoulder
"*Hyrax* \'hi-,raks\ *n. pl hyraxes, also hyraces* [GK 'hyrak-,' 'hyrax,' shrew] any of a family of small ungulate mammals of Africa and the Middle East characterized by thickset body with short legs and ears and rudimentary tail, feet with soft pads and broad nails, and teeth of which the molars resemble those of the rhinoceros and the incisors those of rodents — called also *coney, dassie.*" (*Webster's Collegiate Dictionary,* Tenth Edition)

David Ireland tells me that in East Africa hyraxes are considered pests, apt to be shot on sight, their pelts strung together for rugs.

Enid, Countess of Kenmare, had lived in Kenya; in later years, at her villa La Fiorentina in St. Jean-Cap Ferrat, she used to carry one such animal, also known as a "bush baby," on her shoulder. Charged with having murdered the Earl of Kenmare as well as Lord Furness, her husband before him, she was acquitted both times. By the time I met her, in St. Jean in 1958, she was known in some circles as "Lady Killmore."

None of these details, however, bears directly on the poem.

History at Night
Larry Kert and Carol Lawrence played the romantic leads in the original Broadway production of *West Side Story.*

After Heinrich Heine
I was inspired by Frank O'Hara's poem "An Airplane Whistle, After Heine" to find the Heine poem that O'Hara had in mind. It turned out to be this one, from "Poet Songs":

Die Rose, die Lilie, die Taube, die Sonne,
Die liebt ich einst alle in Liebeswonne.
Ich lieb sie nicht mehr, ich liebe alleine.

Die Kleine, die Feine, die Reine, die Eine;
Sie selber, aller Liebe Bronne,
Ist Rose und Lilie und Taube und Sonne

There is an "error" in my translation — "ich liebe alleine" says "I love alone," which doesn't ring true in English. O'Hara in his poem had the genius to ring up "airplane" for "alleine" and therefore not to pretend, as I have, to be writing an early Romantic lyric. (The original is one of a sequence that Robert Schumann would set glowingly later).

Stains of Stalin
Josef Stalin's identity here, signaled by the title and some of what follows, is analogous to a paper-cutout doll, or the Infant Jesus of Prague, a 16th-century life-size wax figure in the Church of Mary Victor, whose elaborate robes are changed on special days by the Order of English Virgins.

Camera Obscura
The word "disturbation" is Arthur C. Danto's invention. Danto first used it apropos performance art in 1985. In his essay "Bad Aesthetic Times," 1989, Danto writes: "My concept of disturbation is derived from its natural English rhyme, where images have physical consequences — fantasies are transformed into orgasms and hence into feelings of release and peace (when not infected by guilt). Disturbation exploits artistic means to social and moral change, and it is often part of its strategy that the performance artist, when a feminist, vest herself with attributes opposed to commonplace notions of femininity: her art is funky, aggressive, confrontational, flagrant, shocking, daring, extreme and meant to be sensed as dangerous . . ."

The Recital
Written for the catalogue accompanying Eric Fonteneau's exhibition in February 2000 at Southern Exposure, San Francisco. The original title was "À Quoi Bon? / What's the Use?" — a reference to Charles Baudelaire's *Salon of 1846*.

La Poésie Blanche
"La poésie blanche," the poetry of whiteness, is mostly (but not exclusively) French contemporary writing that extends from Mallarmé in its fascination with silence — indicated by large areas of blank paper between words or lines of verse.

Memoir Bay
The Right Bank Cafe still exists on Madison Avenue near Sixty-Ninth Street in New York. Elizabeth Ashley, née Elizabeth Cole, worked as a waitress there in the late 1950s. The phrasing in the last line is anachronistic.